Lovable BABY ANIMALS
COLORING BOOK

MARTY NOBLE

DOVER PUBLICATIONS
GARDEN CITY, NEW YORK

Nature lovers will enjoy coloring this beautiful collection of baby animals in their native habitats. The 31 illustrations feature realistic portraits of parents and their young, including cheetahs, ducks, elephants, giraffes, horses, koalas, llamas, and pandas. The images are printed on one side only, and the pages are perforated for easy removal and display of your finished artwork.

Bibliographical Note

Lovable Baby Animals Coloring Book is a new work,
first published by Dover Publications in 2022.

International Standard Book Number

ISBN-13: 978-0-486-84974-4
ISBN-10: 0-486-84974-0

Manufactured in the United States of America
84974001   2022
www.doverpublications.com